# Where Do You Live?

## Contents

Written by Janice Vale

# Around the world

The way we live depends a lot on the climate and location of the place we live in. Here are six accounts of life lived by children in different places around the world. Find out what the children do in these places that are similar to the things you do, and the things they do that are very different.

Canada

Jersey

Kenya

Nepal

Tuvalu

Australia

3

# Coober Pedy

Would you like to live in a town where there's a spaceship in the main street? And where the only tree for miles around is made of scrap metal? And where most of the houses are underground? If you would, then come to Coober Pedy, my home town. It's a hot, dry, dusty desert town in South Australia and the spaceship and the tree are leftover props from a movie set!

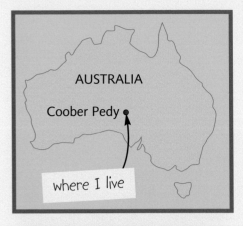

AUSTRALIA

Coober Pedy

where I live

the scrap metal tree

the spaceship

4

I'm Lee and I'm a new Australian. My parents and my gran came here from Cambodia as **refugees**. My dad works as an engineer at the pumping station. He has an important job, making sure that the pumps work. In Coober Pedy it almost never rains so the town depends on the water that's pumped from an underground lake 24 kilometres away. My mum works in an underground tourist hotel and likes meeting all the tourists.

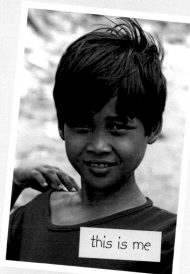

this is me

It wasn't easy for my parents to fit into this way of life. But the 3,500 people here are from 45 different countries so they weren't alone. They both speak English quite well now, but not as well as I do. I can speak Cambodian too, but not as well as my gran!

People have come from all over
the world to mine opals here.
Opals are precious stones used for
jewellery and these are the biggest opal
mines in the world. The only hills you can see
in Coober Pedy are the heaps left over from mining.

opals

an opal mine

my house

But it's not only opals that are found underground. The temperature here in the desert can reach 50 degrees centigrade in summer, so 70% of the houses here are underground. An underground house is cool in two ways! Cool because it's great living in a house that's like a brightly lit cave; and cool because the temperature is much lower than outside. There are shops, museums, an art gallery and even churches underground too.

an underground museum

Some underground houses are very big and a few have swimming pools. Ours is smaller and my bedroom is like a cave. At night I always have a night light on – otherwise it's pitch dark!

7

After school I hang out at the adventure playground with my friend, Bob, and sometimes we go to the **BMX track**. Bob's family loves wheels! They take me off for weekends in their big four-wheel drive. Once they took me to the Dog Fence, 15 kilometres from here. It's a fence that goes across Australia for 5,200 kilometres, and it's the longest man-made thing in the world. It was built to protect sheep from wild Australian dogs, called dingoes.

dingoes

the Dog Fence

Our town's very isolated. It's hundreds of kilometres from anywhere. But there is a road, a railway and an airport, so we aren't cut off and exciting things do happen here. Just recently some top cricketers showed up to teach kids cricket skills. About a hundred kids went and they all want to play cricket for Australia now.

my friends playing cricket

I think we live in a funny sort of place with the spaceship, the scrap metal tree and the underground houses! It might be hot but it's a cool place to live.

Lee

# Kangiqsualujjuaq

Kangiqsualujjuaq

CANADA

where I live

me

My name is Qaaqai. My village is a small group of 126 houses. We have a gas station, a church, a fire station and a huge noisy **diesel** generator to make electricity. We use lots of electricity to keep us warm.

My village is in the **Arctic Circle**, on the eastern side of Ungara Bay, in Quebec, Canada. The temperature is often far below freezing. We are pretty isolated and we don't get many visitors. A big ship brings petrol when the ice melts in summer, and there's a small airport.

my house

We like the cold and we love snow! We often play outside so we have to pile on lots of clothes when we leave our warm houses. I wear a woollen hat, and a down-filled parka with a pocket in the front and a fur-lined hood to shelter my face from the wind. I also wear **caribou** leather mittens lined with sheepskin with fur trim at the wrists. I made them myself, with Mum's help.

my brother Irniq, and sister Puja

me and my friends on our way home in a snowstorm

We really need all our clothes when there's a bad snowstorm and we have
to battle against the wind. I don't like going out when it's like that.
But usually you can't keep me inside! I like playing outside with my friends
on the school's **jungle gym**. We keep it clear of snow. There's a big hill behind
our village and I love sliding down that. I can ski too.

My dad is a fisherman and I also go fishing. In winter we cut holes in the ice and jiggle special hooks down. It was a great day when I caught my first **char**. It was longer than I am wide. If you don't believe me look at the photo I took! This fish would have made a great meal for a polar bear, but I got there first!

my friends Atuat and Nuruiniq

Uncle Atanarjuat

Mum

Sometimes we go camping. We put the big tent on the sled, then all twelve of us pile on, hitch up the snowmobile, and off we go. It's fun.

my dad

my fish!

There's my dad. He's taken his spear to **harpoon** a fish. Maybe we'll get lucky and spear a **narwhal** or a seal. If we get too much caribou or fish on the hunt we store it in the **community** freezer when we get back to the village.

15

Our school has 200 students. It's a new school because an avalanche destroyed our old one. At school we learn three languages: our **Inuit** language, English and French. My big sister walks to school with me. She carries her baby in a pouch on her back. He's going to spend the day in day care. I go home for lunch and Mum makes me a bannock, which is like a fried scone. Yum!

my sister Mitiarjuk, and baby Oki

We do cool things at school. I love using the computers there. When I'm a bit older I'll go on a school camping trip. This year the big kids took two dog teams and three snowmobiles, and they caught lots of fish.

a snowmobile

After school I carry Oki on my back down to the gas station where Mitiarjuk works. When it's dark in the winter we all pile on the couch together and watch TV. Some days we have a big dinner of caribou meat, which I love. Then I go to bed and lie there listening to Arctic wolves howling across the ice.

## Qaaqai

# St Helier

me

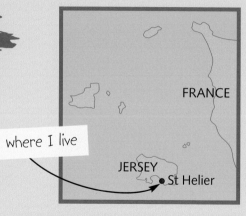

where I live

FRANCE

JERSEY

St Helier

My name's Gemma and I live on the island of Jersey. It's one of the Channel Islands, in the English Channel, between England and France. It's 160 kilometres south of England and 22 kilometres from France so it's much nearer France than England.

You can get here by plane or ferry. Some of the ferries are huge – they look like big buildings in the sea. Most people who come here come for holidays because there's a lot more sun here than there is in England.

CONDOR EXPRESS

www.Condorferries.com

Jersey's a small island, only 14 kilometres by eight kilometres, so you can cycle round it easily in a weekend and see everything! I did that in the Easter holidays, with Dad. We cycled on special roads, called green lanes, which are for slow traffic like bikes, horses and walkers.

my house

About 87,000 people live on Jersey so it's quite crowded and there's lots of traffic. I live in a **parish** called St Helier. It's the main town on the island, on the south coast. There's an old church – built in the 14th century – and there's also an old castle called Elizabeth Castle. It's on a tiny rocky island that's joined to the big island by a **causeway**. When our gran came over on the ferry from Portsmouth to visit us, we took her to the castle.

Elizabeth Castle

Burmese python

orang-utan

There are new things in St Helier as well, like the shops. Saturday is my favourite day of the week because I go shopping, to the library, and best of all, I often visit the zoo. I'm a member of the Dodo Club, which is a special club for children in Jersey. Members get to meet **endangered**, rare animals at the zoo. I've actually met and talked to a **Burmese python** and an orang-utan. They didn't talk to me though!

21

I like my school. After school I do ballet and gymnastics. School's just down the road from the house I live in with Mum. Dad lives in St John, another parish. I stay with him every second weekend and I have my own bedroom in both houses. Every Friday night I go to a restaurant in the middle of town, with Mum and Mum's friend, Dan. We often sit outside and watch the boats in the harbour. On Sundays, Dan sometimes takes us sailing in his boat.

my favourite restaurant

My mum's an accountant and she works in an office. I sometimes visit her office but it's a bit boring. Dad works in an office too. He's a landscape gardener and he works for our parish, St Helier. He decides which flowers to plant in the parks and in August he designs the parish float for the massive parade called the Battle of Flowers. It's on the second Thursday in August and all the floats are decorated with flowers. Thousands of people from all over the world come to Jersey to see the parade.

Gemma

the Battle of Flowers parade

23

# Jora

My name is Pascal. I belong to the Taita tribe and I live in Jora, a small village in Kenya, East Africa. Above our village is Mount Kasigau, our **ancestral home**.

KENYA

Jora

where I live

this is me

To get to our village you drive along the main Nairobi to Mombasa highway, then turn off and follow a winding dirt road for two hours.

my house

We have a small farm called a shamba, three **hectares** in size, where we grow maize, beans and peas to eat. We have a few chickens for eggs, and a goat for milk. Our house is made of sticks, mud and thatched grass. To get water we go to the community village tap and fill a bucket.

Our main food is maize. My mother and sisters pound it into flour and cook it in a big pot on the open fire. Our grinding bowl is the oldest thing we have – it was my great grandmother's.

My mother also cooks for visitors who come to study the animals and plants on the mountain and in the national park. They don't know how much trouble giraffes and elephants cause when they wander through our maize patch and ruin all our hard work.

my mum and sisters. Wachia is trying to grind the maize – she's only two!

26

Another thing that can ruin our maize crop is **drought**. Sometimes the rain just doesn't come. We look up into the blue sky and there are no clouds at all.

One of my brothers is a shopkeeper. He gives us money when the shop is doing well.

When I'm not at school my favourite hobby is soccer. Every evening when it's cooler we gather on the big patch of ground that is our football pitch. It's beaten hard as concrete and it hurts when you fall on it. Ouch!

One of the best things about the high school where I might go one day is that they give out shoes for playing soccer in, and they have a proper soccer pitch.

my friends on our soccer pitch

I should stop talking about soccer now and tell you about my school. Our tribe values education so much that we built our own school. It has ten classrooms and 350 students. The school buildings are simple and basic. No windows. No doors. No floors. We have blackboards and chalk.

my class

At first we are taught in our own language, Kiswahili; then, after two years, we start to learn English.

To move up from one grade to the next you have to pass an examination. It's hard and I worry that I won't pass this year. If I don't I'll have to stay in the same class for the whole of next year.

My family can afford the fee for primary school but it will be more difficult when I want to go to Moi High School in Kasigau. Every year the two top students from our school get their fees paid for the high school, and I hope I get one of these scholarships. If I do, it will be a great sacrifice for my family because the high school is a boarding school and I wouldn't be able to help out on our shamba.

But the school has some computers and solar panels to generate electricity to run them. That, and the soccer, makes me really want to go to high school.

Pascal

Moi High School

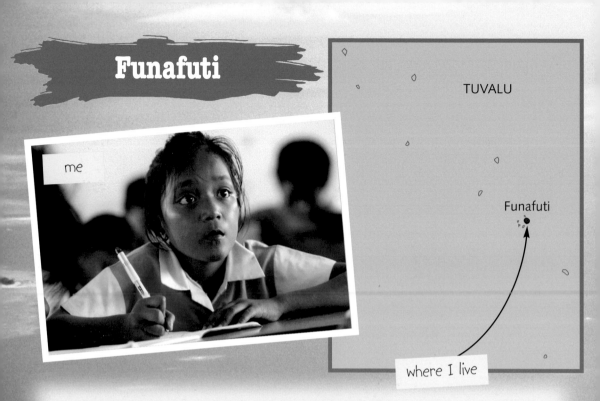

# Funafuti

TUVALU

Funafuti

me

where I live

I'm Emeli. My home is in Funafuti. It's a small place but it's actually the capital of my country, Tuvalu. Tuvalu is one of the least populated countries in the world, with only 11,500 people. But it's a string of about 34 tiny islands, spread over a large area of the Pacific Ocean. Most of the islands are like Funafuti – atolls made of **coral**. They are flat, low-lying crescents or circles of coral. In the middle is a lagoon where the water is shallow and calm and full of fish. It's our playground.

Our town has an airstrip, a new government building and a supermarket. Planes fly here from Fiji. Our island's lucky because big ships can come into our lagoon to unload supplies and take our crop of coconuts.

If we want to visit people on other islands in Tuvalu we have to go by boat. There's a boat that goes round the islands every two weeks, stopping at every island for about an hour. It takes three days to get to the southern islands, and four days to get to the northernmost ones. I told you Tuvalu was spread out!

one of the big ships unloading supplies

My father used to take our family's **outrigger** canoe through the surf out into the ocean to catch big fish. But at the moment he's gone to another island to work. There's very little work on Tuvalu.

my family spearfishing on the lagoon

While he's away my uncle uses our canoe and he takes my elder brother out with him. Each family has work they have to do for the community. It's called salanga. Our family's task is to fish. When my uncle comes in with lots of fish we share it with everyone else.

Today the whole family is at home because it's Sunday. The canoe is pulled up and covered with mats. No one works on Sunday. Everyone goes to church and then we eat a big feast. We are having pork, coconut cream, **taro**, bananas and **papaya**. When we've eaten we'll relax for a while on platforms in the shade of the **breadfruit** trees; then we'll play a ball game called te ano. Two teams line up, facing each other, boys and girls, men and women – anyone can play. They throw a heavy ball back and forth very fast. You get very hot playing in the sun!

people in my village playing te ano

My elder brother likes riding around on his motorbike when he's not fishing. When I'm not in school I love dancing. I'm learning the traditional **fatele.** We perform these dances when we're greeting visitors and when there's an important holiday, like National Children's Day in August. We all celebrate that!

fatele dancers welcoming new visitors to our island

34

Our island is warm. The average temperature is 29 degrees centigrade and rain falls on half the days of the year. November to April is the hurricane season when we can get very strong winds that bend the coconut palms right over. But we can cope with hurricanes. There's one new thing, though, that has us all worried.

Because our island is so low – the highest point is only five metres above the ocean – we are all worried about the sea level rising. A **tide-gauge** has been set up and it shows that for the last ten years the sea level has been rising steadily. Two years ago our taro crop was ruined when sea water seeped up into the soil and we had a salty lake where we should have had a garden.

Everyone gave us some of their taro and we all helped to build up the sea wall. But what will we do if the sea keeps rising?

Emeli

the sea wall we built

# Nangi

My name is Vina and I live on top of the world in Nangi, a village in Nepal, 2,260 metres above sea level. Above our village are two of the highest mountains in the world, Annapurna and Dhaulagiri.

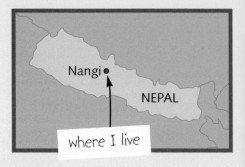

Nangi

NEPAL

where I live

this is me

my house

If you want to visit me this is what you have to do: fly to Katmandu, the capital of Nepal, then take a seven hour bus ride or a 35 minute plane trip to Pokhara, the second largest city in Nepal. From Pokhara travel by bus for three to five hours to Beni, the nearest major town to Nangi. Then you have to walk, for six to nine hours, and it's all uphill!

We like going to festivals at the village next to us. It takes two hours to walk there, but it's worth the wait. There are great processions through the streets, with music and lots of colour, dancing and noise. I like dressing up for festivals and wearing jewellery, and sometimes I have a rice **bindi** applied to my forehead. We make offerings in the temple every day but we have our own mountain gods too.

my mum

my brothers Adesh and Mani

Mani has a rice bindi on his forehead.

My auntie Mala is making dal bhat.

I will make you dal bhat when you arrive, tired from your walk. This is our main food. It's a dish made of rice and lentils, with garlic, onions and spices. We'll probably give you potatoes with it. And, as your visit will be a special occasion for us, we'll have a stew of one of our chickens, rabbits, goats or sheep for meat. We don't eat beef because cows are holy to **Hindus**. If you come in the autumn we could eat peaches, plums and apples, and we could go hunting for wild fruits or mushrooms on the hills. But bring your raincoat. The **monsoon** winds bring lots of rain at that time of year.

Don't come in winter. We get a lot of snow and stay inside most of the time. My mother thinks you should come in March or April when the rhododendron forests are in bloom.

You won't be able to meet my eldest brother because he's joined the Indian Army. We belong to the Pun Magar tribe and we have a tradition here that men who pass the test become **Gurkha** soldiers. They send money home. At the moment, from the 800 people in the village, about 40 men are in the Indian Army and 75 are retired soldiers.

my brother Shyam

If you aren't in the army you are a farmer. We have an ox to plough the field for us. Everything else we do ourselves. Our farm is a series of terraces, like steps, up the steep mountainside. We grow potatoes, corn, millet, barley, beans and buckwheat. We also grow pumpkins and cucumbers.

my house

I go to school at Himanchal High School with my little brother and sister. Lots of children come here to school from other villages. There are about 350 students of all ages and 18 teachers. You can do all kinds of subjects, even computing. Last week we had a **working bee** at the school to help level a new playing field. If you'd been here you could have joined in! My little brother proudly carried his share of stones up the hill for the retaining wall. I had a new radio with me, which I bought with money my brother sent. So we all listened to Indian pop music. It was a great day. Come and join us soon!

Vina

# Glossary

**ancestral home**   a place which was lived in many years ago by members of the same family or tribe that lives there now

**Arctic Circle**   the imaginary circle around the Earth, with the North Pole inside the circle

**bindi**   usually a red dot on a Hindu's forehead, but it can be applied in different ways

**BMX track**   a rough track or obstacle course for performing stunts on a bicycle

**breadfruit**   a round fruit, with a texture like bread, which can be cooked and eaten

**Burmese python**   a very large snake that squeezes its prey until it stops breathing

**caribou**   an Arctic reindeer

**causeway**   a raised path or road which crosses water, marshes or sand

**char**   a fish, similar to a trout, found in cold lakes and northern seas

**community**   a group of people living together in one place

**coral**   a hard red, pink or white substance built by tiny sea creatures

**diesel**   a heavy fuel used in trains, buses, lorries and some cars

**drought**   a long period without rain

**endangered**   in danger of disappearing

**fatele**   a traditional dance, used to celebrate leaders and other important people

| | |
|---|---|
| **Gurkha** | soldiers in the Indian army |
| **harpoon** | to spear with a harpoon, which is a barbed spear attached to a rope |
| **hectares** | units of area; one hectare equals 10,000 square metres |
| **Hindus** | people who believe in Hinduism, an Indian religion that has many gods and involves the belief that people have another life on earth after death |
| **Inuit** | an Eskimo or the Eskimo language |
| **jungle gym** | a climbing frame |
| **monsoon** | the rainy season |
| **narwhal** | an Arctic whale, with a black-spotted whitish skin; the male has a long spiral tusk |
| **outrigger** | a framework attached to the outside of a canoe to stop it tipping over |
| **papaya** | a sweet yellow fruit with small black seeds |
| **parish** | a small area of a town; each parish in a town is connected to a different church |
| **refugees** | people who have run away from their home to find safety somewhere else |
| **taro** | a big starchy root vegetable |
| **tide-gauge** | an instrument used to measure the movement of the tide |
| **working bee** | a group of people who do voluntary work to help others |

# Pronunciation guide

| | |
|---|---|
| Dhaulagiri | (darl-gi-ri) |
| fatele | (fa-telly) |
| Funafuti | (fun-a-foo-tee) |
| Inuit | (inn-oo-it) |
| Kangiqsualujjuaq | (kang-ick-joo-ah-lu-jooak) |
| Kasigau | (kas-i-gow) |
| Kiswahili | (key-swa-heely) |
| Moi | (moy) |
| Nairobi | (ny-row-be) |
| Pokhara | (pok-har-a) |
| Quebec | (kwe-beck) |
| Taita | (ty-ter) |
| te ano | (tay-ar-no) |
| Tuvalu | (too-val-oo) |

# Index

# Where do you live?

| This is me | My name | Where I live | Location |
|:---:|:---:|:---:|:---:|
| | **Lee** | Coober Pedy | Australia |
| | **Qaaqai** | Kangiqsualujjauq | Canada |
| | **Gemma** | St Helier | Jersey |
| | **Pascal** | Jora | Kenya |
| | **Emeli** | Funafuti | Tuvalu |
| | **Vina** | Nangi | Nepal |

| My hobbies and interests | My parents' occupations | Fascinating facts |
|---|---|---|
| • playing at the adventure playground<br>• BMX | Dad is an engineer.<br>Mum works in a hotel. | • We live in underground caves.<br>• We have the biggest opal mines in the world.<br>• It can be 50 degrees centigrade in the summer. |
| • playing in the snow<br>• fishing | Dad is a fisherman.<br>Mum is a homemaker. | • The temperature is often below freezing.<br>• We fish and hunt and store food in the community freezer.<br>• In winter, we cut holes in the ice to fish. |
| • visiting the zoo with the Dodo Club<br>• ballet and gymnastics | Dad is a landscape gardener.<br>Mum is an accountant. | • You can cycle right round the island in a weekend.<br>• Every August we have a parade called the Battle of Flowers. |
| • playing soccer<br>• computers | My parents have their own farm.<br>Mum also cooks for visitors. | • Giraffes and elephants often trample on our crops.<br>• We built our school ourselves. |
| • playing te ano<br>• dancing | Dad works on another island.<br>Mum is a homemaker. | • Tuvalu is a string of 34 islands.<br>• We all have to work for the community.<br>• It rains on half the days of the year. |
| • dressing up for festivals<br>• listening to music | My parents are farmers. | • It is 2,260 metres above sea level.<br>• We stay inside most of the winter.<br>• We don't eat beef because cows are holy to Hindus. |

# ✿ Ideas for guided reading ✿

**Learning objectives:** to prepare for factual research by reviewing what is known, what is needed, what is available and where one might search; scan texts in print or on screen to locate key words or phrases, useful headings; make short notes e.g. by abbreviating ideas, selecting key words, listing or in diagrammatic form; use alternative words and expressions which are more accurate or interesting than common choices; develop scripts based on improvisation

**Curriculum links:** Geography: Knowledge and understanding of places; describe and identify what places are like; describe where places are; a contrasting locality overseas; village settler; Citizenship: Living in a diverse world

**Interest words:** ancestral home, Arctic circle, breadfruit, Burmese python, caribou, causeway, char, fatele, Ghurkha, hectares, Hindi, Inuit, narwhal, papaya, refugees, taro, tide gauge

**Resources:** paper and pens, the internet

## Getting started

*This book can be read over two or more guided reading sessions.*

- Read the covers and quickly scan inside to decide the purpose of the text.

- Ask for a volunteer to read aloud pp2–3.

- Explain to the children that each of them is to read about one child in order to report back to the others.

## Reading and responding

- Ask a volunteer to say a couple of things they have found out about their child.

- With reference to the book, the rest of the group should take turns to volunteer similar information about their chosen child (e.g. *school, hobbies, family*).

- Children read on silently, making notes about their chosen child as necessary. Praise those who start to make notes on the country the child lives in.